Backyard SCIENTIST

BACKYARD BOTANY EXPERIMENTS

Alix Wood

PowerKiDS press

New York

Published in 2019 by Rosen Publishing
29 East 21st Street, New York, NY 10010

Produced for Rosen Publishing by Alix Wood Books
Designed by Alix Wood
Editor: Eloise Macgregor
Projects devised and photographed by Kevin Wood

Cover, 1, 4, 5, 6 far right, 7 top right and bottom © Adobe Stock Images;
all other photos © Kevin Wood

Cataloging-in-Publication Data
Names: Wood, Alix.
Title: Backyard botany experiments / Alix Wood.
Description: New York : PowerKids Press, 2019. | Series: Backyard scientist | Includes glossary
and index.
Identifiers: LCCN ISBN 9781538337349 (pbk.) | ISBN 9781538337332 (library bound) |
ISBN 9781538337356 (6 pack)
Subjects: LCSH: Plants--Experiments--Juvenile literature. | Botany--Experiments--Juvenile
literature.
Classification: LCC QK52.6 W64 2019 | DDC 580.78--dc23

Printed in the United States of America

CPSIA compliance information: Batch # CS18PK: For further information contact Rosen Publishing, New York, New York at 1-800-237-9932.

Contents

What Is Botany?

Botany is the science of how plants work. Botanists study everything from the tiniest seeds to the tallest trees. Plants are important. People depend on plants for many things. They can give us food, and provide food for birds and animals. We can make clothing from plants, build houses, and create drugs to make us better when we are sick. Plants even help supply the **oxygen** we breathe!

Parts of a Plant

seeds
Help the flower **reproduce**.

flower
Attracts insects and makes seeds.

leaves
Soak up sunlight to make food for the plant.

stem
Supports the plant and carries **nutrients** and water to the leaves and flowers.

roots
Soak up water and nutrients, and secure the plant in the ground

4

Setting Up Your Backyard Laboratory

Find an outside space that you can use to do these experiments. Some of them are pretty messy! Remember to check with whomever owns the space that it is OK to do your experiments there. You may want to find a picnic table to work on.

You should be able to find most of the things you will need around your home or yard. You may need to buy some small items, so check the "You Will Need" section before you start a project.

BE SCIENTIFIC

Botanists use the scientific method, a process used by scientists to study the world around them. Botanists first ask a question, such as "Can plants grow without sunlight?" Then, they test to see if their idea is true. They may set up an experiment with some plants given sunlight, and some not. When they examine the results, they can decide if their idea was proven correct.

STAYING SAFE

The experiments in this book have been specially chosen because they are fun and relatively safe, but you must still be careful. Ask an adult to help you. Follow all warnings. Wear any suggested protective clothing, and be careful. MOST IMPORTANT—wash your hands thoroughly, particularly after touching soil or eggshells.

Grow Beans from a Bean

Plants are really amazing. Did you know that most plants can reproduce themselves by creating seeds. Inside each seed is a baby plant called an **embryo**. Try planting a bean seed and then watch it grow into a fully grown bean plant.

YOU WILL NEED:

- a see-through container
- an outside space or large flowerpot
- compost
- some bean seeds
- a long stick

1 Place some compost in a see-through container. Push three bean seeds around the edge of the container, so you can see them through the side.

2 Water the compost and wait. After about a week you should start to see roots grow out of your seed. Then a shoot should start to appear.

3

Once your seedling has leaves, and the weather is warm, plant it in the ground or a large flowerpot. Give each bean a stick to climb up as it grows. Water it regularly.

4

Once plants mature, they make flowers. Insects, such as bees, are attracted to flowers, and help spread the **pollen**, which fertilizes the flower. This causes the flower to produce seeds.

WHAT'S HAPPENING?

A flowering plant's life cycle allows it to reproduce. The flowers that grow on the plant create seeds. These beans that have grown on your runner bean plant contain runner bean seeds. Cut open the green pod, and you will see the seeds inside. You can plant one of the seeds and make a new runner bean plant!

Plants Create Water

Trees release a lot of water on a hot day through a process known as **transpiration**. Transpiration cools the plant and also helps it move water around itself. Some scientists think that more water enters the air from plants transpiring than from **evaporation** from the surface of the ocean!

1

Find a tree or shrub with some green leaves in easy reach. On a sunny day, put a clear plastic bag over some of the leaves.

2

Tie the bag tightly to the branch using a plastic tie or some string. You need to prevent any air from being able to escape.

3

Wait around fifteen minutes and then look at the bag. You should start to see a few water droplets forming.

4

After an hour, the bag should be full of **condensation**. Using a measuring jug, measure the amount of water produced by different trees.

WHAT'S HAPPENING?

Water from the leaves condenses when it reaches the surface of the plastic bag. As the bag is tied tight, the water cannot escape. People trained in survival techniques sometimes use this trick to create drinking water!

Watch Flowers Drink

When a plant's leaves and flower petals lose water to the air, the water must be replaced. Plants pull liquid from the ground up through their stems and to their flowers and leaves. If you add dye to a plant's water supply, you can see the colored water gradually reach the petals in this cool experiment. Try it.

YOU WILL NEED:

- four kinds of food coloring
- a white flowering plant (we used a carnation)
- scissors
- water
- four jars or glasses of water

ADULT HELP NEEDED

1

Put several drops of food color into each glass of water. Make the solutions a strong color.

2

Using the scissors, trim the end off each flower stem. You may need an adult to help you.

3

Place a cut flower in each of the containers of colored water. Leave the flowers for several days.

After a couple of days the colored water should have changed the color of the petals. Our red dye worked best. Which color worked the best for you?

WHAT'S HAPPENING?

The plant stem acts a little like a straw, pulling the liquid up to the flower petals. It does this because water evaporating from the leaves, buds, and petals pulls water up the stem of the plant. This water movement process through tiny tubes is called **capillary action**.

Seeds in the Wind

Have you ever wondered how seeds spread themselves around? Some seeds are designed to use wind power. Make this seed spinner and see how these seeds can fly through the air.

1

Cut a strip of paper 1 1/2 inches (4 cm) wide by 8 1/2 inches (22 cm) long.

2

Fold the strip into thirds. Crease the folds. Unfold and cut a slit from one end to 1/2 inch (1 cm) from one fold.

3

Make two 1/2-inch (1 cm) cuts on both sides along that fold. Fold the paper up along the crease, and fold the sides inward on the two small cuts.

4

Secure the bottom of your seed spinner with a paper clip. Fold out the wings and it is ready to fly.

WHAT'S HAPPENING?

Wind power helps take seeds away from the parent plant. The seeds have a better chance of growing into healthy plants if they're not overcrowded. Many plants use animals or birds to spread their seeds. How? They eat the plant's fruit and then poop out the seeds!

Drop your seed spinner from a safe, high place. Watch it spin as it falls to the ground.

Room to Grow

Do plants really need room to grow? Too many seeds all in one place will compete for food. If you look at the instructions on seed packets they recommend you space out the seeds when you plant them, or thin the seedlings out once they start to grow. Try this experiment to understand why.

1

Fill two identical pots with some compost. Moisten the compost with water.

2

In one pot, plant your seeds the recommended distance apart, taken from the instructions on the packet.

3

Fill the other pot with a handful of seeds, clumped together in the pot.

4

Put both pots in a warm, sunny spot. Watch how they grow. Which plants do you think will grow the strongest?

WHAT'S HAPPENING?

The overcrowded seeds started to sprout but soon died. There were too many all competing for the same space and nutrients. The nicely spaced seeds thrived.

Make Compost

Compost helps improve the soil by adding **minerals**, particularly **carbon** and **nitrogen**. It also attracts earthworms and other useful insects. It's easy to make your own compost, and cheaper than buying it from the store. You will need some patience though, as it takes around a month to make.

YOU WILL NEED:

- plastic bottle
- scissors
- some tape
- some moist soil
- eggshells
- grass clippings and leaves
- green kitchen waste
- tea bags and coffee grounds

ADULT HELP NEEDED

1 Gather together your compost ingredients. Rinse out your bottle, screw the top on, and take off the label.

2 Ask an adult to cut around the bottle, a third of the way down. Leave a small piece uncut, so it has a flip top.

3

Place a layer of moist soil in the bottom of the bottle. Then add a layer of kitchen waste.

4

Add layers of grass, leaves, eggshells, green kitchen waste, and tea and coffee grinds. Between each layer add a thin layer of soil.

5

Once full, tape the top in place. Put the bottle in a sunny place. If it steams up, open the lid and let the compost dry a little. If it looks dry, add a little water. Roll the bottle every day to mix the compost. The compost is ready when it is brown and crumbly.

WHAT'S HAPPENING?

The best compost has a mix of brown, carbon-rich materials such as old leaves, and green nitrogen-rich materials such as grass and kitchen scraps. The soil adds worms and insects that break down the materials. Don't use meat, fat, dairy products, or pet waste.

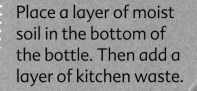

Grow Space Food

So you need soil to grow plants, right? Not necessarily! Growing plants without soil is known as hydroponics. The National Aeronautics and Space Administration (NASA) is even looking at how hydroponics might help us grow food in space. Try this experiment and grow your own space plants.

1 Using the marker, draw a line around the middle of the bottle. Ask an adult to help you cut the bottle in two. Fill the bottom half with water.

2 Put a large piece of sock halfway through the soda bottle top. It needs to fully block the hole.

3

Mix a cup of perlite with a cup of peat moss in a bowl. Put the mix in the bottle top. Pour a cup of water into the mix.

4

Place the top upside down into the bottom half of the bottle. The sock needs to be in the water. The sock must also block the hole, so no mix falls through.

WHAT'S HAPPENING?

The sock soaks up the water to keep the plants' roots moist. The mix gives the plants all the nutrients that they need.

5

Drop some lettuce seeds in the bottle top and cover them with some mix. Wrap the bottle top in cling wrap. After a week, some lettuce seedlings should appear.

Cloning a Cabbage

Plants don't only reproduce using seeds. Strawberry plants produce **runners**, stems that grow a new strawberry plant at the end. Some plants can be **cloned** from cuttings, too. A clone is a copy. Apple trees are cloned by putting a cutting of an old apple tree onto a new stem. Try this experiment and clone yourself a new cabbage plant!

YOU WILL NEED:

- paper towels
- two ziplock bags
- scissors
- a Napa cabbage
- a cutting board
- a knife
- marker
- water

ADULT HELP NEEDED

1

Take two ziplock bags. Using the marker, label one "leaf" and the other "stem." You can make labels, or write on the bags.

2

Fold two sheets of paper towel three times, into rectangles. Wet the towels with water until they are quite damp. Put a towel in each bag.

3

Remove a leaf from the cabbage. Ask an adult to cut off a section of the stem, from near where the roots would have been.

4

Put the leaf and the stem inside the towel in their bags. Make sure the bags have air in them. Close the bags and leave them in a warm, sunny place.

Look in the bags after a week. The stem should have grown small roots. What happened to the leaf?

WHAT'S HAPPENING?

The **cells** near the cabbage's root can grow new roots. The new cabbage plant is a clone—that is, exactly the same as the one the stem came from. Some plants clone more easily than others. Test out some different vegetables. Can you find any others that clone easily?

Twisting to the Light

Have you ever noticed how plants tend to bend toward the light as they grow? Plants grow as their cells get longer, or divide into new cells. Cells that are away from direct light grow faster than cells on the light side of the plant stem. This causes the plant stems to bend toward the light.

YOU WILL NEED:

- plant seedling in pot
- shoebox with lid
- water
- masking tape
- pencil
- scissors
- a sheet of card stock

ADULT HELP NEEDED

1

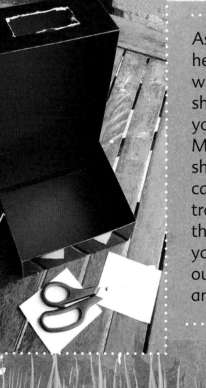

Ask an adult to help you cut a window in one short side of your shoebox. Make two shelves out of card stock by tracing around the short side of your box. Cut out the shape and cut it in half.

2

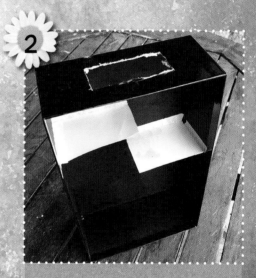

Tape the shelves inside the shoebox as shown. Leave enough room at the bottom for your flowerpot and plant.

3

Put your seedling into the bottom of the box. The window must be at the top of the box. Put on the box lid.

WHAT'S HAPPENING?

A plant's ability to move toward light is called **phototropism**. Moving toward light gives the leaves the maximum sunlight energy. A green chemical in leaves, called **chlorophyll**, changes sunlight into energy and sugar. A plant kept in a dark place loses its green color because sunlight also helps to make chlorophyll.

4

Put your box in a sunny place. Keep the soil moist. After a week your plant should have weaved its way around the shelves to find the sunlight.

Which Way Is Up?

Plants grow toward the sunlight, but this is not the only reason that they grow upward. Plants can sense **gravity**, and actually tell which way is up! Try this experiment and hang a plant upside down in full sunlight. It should start to turn upward.

YOU WILL NEED:

- two sponges
- a small plant
- some string
- a pair of scissors
- water
- a thumbtack

1 Pour water over the two sponges until they are moist.

2 Find a small potted plant. Beans work well. We used a sweet pea plant. Take the plant out of its pot. Remove most of the soil.

3

Sandwich the roots of the plant between the two damp sponges.

4

Tie the sponges together with string as shown. Hang the plant upside down from a thumbtack in a sunny spot.

Keep the sponges watered. In a few days the plant will turn and grow upright.

WHAT'S HAPPENING?

Scientists think gravity makes the heavy **starch** inside plant cells fall to the bottom of each cell. This shows the plant which way is up. NASA has done experiments in space showing that plants grow in spirals when there is little or no gravity.

Make Some Fertilizer

Good soil contains all the nutrients a plant needs, but over time the goodness get used up. Gardeners add fertilizers to make the soil full of nutrients again. Try making your own liquid fertilizer. Ask permission before you do this experiment, as it will make your lawn look odd for a while!

YOU WILL NEED:

- gardening gloves
- a bucket
- water
- sticks
- nettles, or comfrey, or eggshells, coffee grounds, and fish tank water

nettle   comfrey

1

Put on some good gardening gloves. Pick some nettles or comfrey leaves. Place them in a bucket of water.

2

If you can't find nettles or comfrey, you can use water from a freshwater fish tank mixed with coffee grounds and crushed eggshells.

3

Put your bucket outside, somewhere far from people as it will start to smell! Leave it for two weeks.

WHAT'S HAPPENING?

Nettle and comfrey plants have long roots which allow them to absorb more nutrients from the soil than other plants. Comfrey contains the minerals nitrogen, phosphorus, and potassium. Nettles, tea, and coffee grounds are rich in nitrogen. Eggshells are rich in calcium.

4

Mark out a square with sticks. Water the area with your fertilizer.

5

Wait a couple of weeks. Lift the sticks. Can you see the difference in your fertilized patch of grass?

Test Your Botany Know-How!

Are you a botany genius? Test yourself with these questions. The answers are on page 29.

1. What is botany?

a) the study of robots b) the study of plants c) the study of fish

2. How do insects help plants reproduce?

a) they help spread pollen from the flowers
b) they eat the plant's leaves
c) they burrow into its roots

3. What is transpiration?

a) how a plant breathes
b) when a plant makes a new plant
c) when a plant releases water from its leaves

4. Which part of the plant takes water from the roots to the leaves and flowers?

a) the stem b) the seeds c) the petals

5. All plants must have soil to grow?

a) true b) false

6. In what ways do plant seeds get spread around?

a) by the wind

b) by animals and birds eating their fruit

c) both a and b

7. Why do plants need to spread their seeds around?

a) because flower beds will look prettier that way

b) because seeds need their own space and nutrients to grow

c) because the plants don't want them anymore

8. Which of these should you not use to make compost?

a) green kitchen scraps   b) eggshells   c) a hamburger

9. What is a clone?

a) a type of cabbage

b) a plant exactly like its parent plant

c) a type of soil

10. What is the chemical in leaves that makes them look green?

a) chlorophyll   b) oxygen   c) nitrogen

Glossary

capillary action How liquid moves up a plant's stalk.

carbon An element found in the bodies of living things.

cells One of the basic building blocks of living things.

chlorophyll The green coloring matter of plants.

cloned Grown from a single body cell of its parent.

condensation Water vapor in the air that has condensed from a gas back into a liquid.

embryo A tiny young plant within a seed.

evaporation The process of passing off into vapor from a liquid state.

gravity A force of attraction between bodies due to their mass.

minerals Naturally occurring substances in the ground.

nitrogen An element that forms a part of all living tissues.

nutrients Substances needed for healthy growth.

oxygen An element necessary for life.

phototropism A movement toward the light.

pollen A mass of tiny particles in a flower that fertilize the seeds.

reproduce To produce offspring.

runners A slender creeping stem from the base of a plant.

starch A carbohydrate stored in plants.

transpiration The process by which plants give off water vapor through their leaves.

For More Information

Anders, Mason. *Plant Cells.* North Mankato, MN: Capstone Press, 2018.

Cornell, Kari. *Dig In!: 12 Easy Gardening Projects Using Kitchen Scraps.* Minneapolis, MN: Millbrook Press, 2018.

Dorion, Christiane. *How Plants and Trees Work: A Hands-On Guide to the Natural World.* Somerville, MA: Candlewick Press, 2017.

Stewart, Melissa. *A Seed Is the Start.* Washington, DC: National Geographic Kids, 2018.

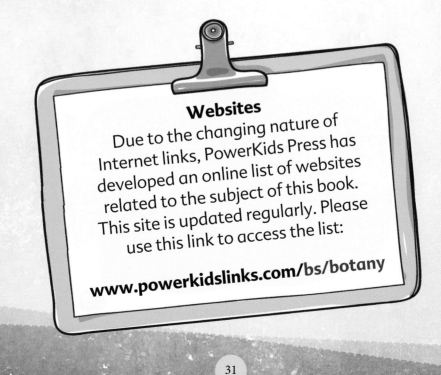

Websites

Due to the changing nature of Internet links, PowerKids Press has developed an online list of websites related to the subject of this book. This site is updated regularly. Please use this link to access the list:

www.powerkidslinks.com/bs/botany

Index